photo**word**book

Farm animals

Sue Barraclough

First published in 2007 by Wayland

This paperback edition published in 2010 by Wayland

Copyright © Wayland 2007

Wayland
338 Euston Road
London NW1 3BH

Wayland Australia
Level 17/207 Kent Street
Sydney, NSW 2000

Design: Natascha Frensch
Typography: Natascha Frensch
Read Regular (European Community Design Registration 2003)
Read Regular and Read Xheavy copyright © Natascha Frensch 2001-2006

Editor: Joyce Bentley
Picture research: Sue Barraclough

ISBN 978 0 7502 6164 7

Printed in China

Wayland is a division of Hachette Children's Books, an Hachette UK company.
www.hachette.co.uk

Acknowledgements: Cover © Franz Lemmens/The Image Bank/
Getty; p1, 13, 22 © Momatiuk - Eastcott/Corbis; Pp 2-3 Digital
Vision; Pp 4-5: © David Frazier/Corbis; p 7, 22 © Julie Habel/
Corbis; pp 8-9 © Chinch Gryniewicz; Ecoscene/Corbis;
pp 10-11 A Bartel/Taxi/Getty; p 12 © Owaki - Kulla/
Corbis; p 15, 22 Paul McCormick/The Image Bank/
Getty; p 16 Hans Reinhard/Taxi/Getty;
p17 © Tom Stewart/Corbis; pp 18-19, 22
Franz Lemmens/The Image Bank/Getty;
pp 20-21 © Hans Reinhard/zefa/
Corbis

2

Contents

3

farm

This is a **farm**.

Some animals live on farms.

COW

This is a **COW**.

A baby **COW** is called a calf.

sheep

These are **sheep**.

A sheep's woolly coat keeps it warm.

9

lamb

This is a **lamb**.

A **lamb** is a baby sheep.

farmer

This is a **farmer**.

The **farmer** feeds the cows.

horse

This is a **horse**.

A baby **horse**
is called a foal.

hen

This is a **hen**.

The **hen** has some chicks.

pig

This is a **pig**.

This **pig** is eating a flower.

piglet

These are **piglets**.

A **piglet** is a baby pig.

goat

This is a goat.

A baby goat is called a kid.

duck

This is a duck.

The duck has lots of fluffy ducklings!

21

Picture quiz

Can you find these baby animals in
the book?

kid

calf

foal

chicks

What pages are they on?

Index quiz

The index is on page 24.
Use the index and pictures
to answer these questions.

1. Which pages show **sheep**?
   What keeps a sheep warm?

2. Which page shows a **pig**?
   What colour is the flower?

3. Which page shows a **farmer**?
   What is the farmer doing?

4. Which page shows a **duck**?
   How many ducklings can you count?

Index

Answers

Picture quiz: The kid is on page 19. The calf is on page 7. The foal is on page 13. The chicks are on page 15.

Index quiz: Pages 8 & 9, a woolly coat; 2. Page 16, yellow; 3. Page 12, feeding the cows; 4. Page 20, 8